GIVING SORROW WORDS:

POEMS OF STRENGTH AND SOLACE

GIVE SORROW WORDS:
THE GRIEF THAT DOES NOT SPEAK
WHISPERS THE O'ER-FRAUGHT HEART
AND BIDS IT BREAK

WILLIAM SHAKESPEARE
MACBETH, ACT IV, SCENE 3

CONTENTS

FOREWORD

On the morning of September 11, 2001, when terrorist-hijacked planes crashed into the World Trade Center Towers and the Pentagon, poetry began pouring into the offices of the National Association for Poetry Therapy (NAPT). Across geographic, ethnic and cultural lines friends and strangers reached out with one voice, and that voice was poetry.

One of NAPT's key purposes—to offer poetic resources for comfort, healing and growth to all who need them—was brought into sharp focus in those mid-September days. Within a week of the terrorist attacks, we posted on the NAPT website some of the poems we had gathered. The NAPT Board of Directors unanimously agreed to support the publication of a collection of original and previously published poems that spoke not only to the phenomenon of 9/11, but also to the broader experience of catastrophic loss and complicated grief. The Board also concurred that this collection must be available at no cost to anyone and everyone who could use it.

The NAPT Foundation, the work of which is to financially support NAPT and the field of poetry therapy, immediately offered the funding to launch the project. NAPT's Publications Chair, Karen vanMeenen, and Special Projects Chair, Charles Rossiter, began work.

While the editors sorted and sifted through scores of poems, stories started streaming in about the impact of the temporary collection. The principal of a Catholic middle school wrote to say that every one of her teachers had been given copies of the poems, and all were using them as springboards for discussion. "Even our science and math teachers are using them," she said. "Reading one of the poems over the intercom in the morning has become an honor that the kids line up for. Do you have any more?"

Therapists, doctors and counselors by the dozens called and wrote to report that even though they had never before used poetry with their clients, even though they didn't themselves read or write or understand or even *like* poetry, they found that the poems inspired healing work of startling depth.

Individuals wrote and called to share how the poems had reached in and touched something that wanted to be soothed or shaken loose. They shared their own poems written in response, and many times they told stories of past wounds or griefs or sadnesses that somehow seemed better now.

Registered and Certified Poetry Therapists in Manhattan; Washington, DC; Boston and elsewhere around the country began working with survivors of the victims of the terrorist attacks. They infused these poems with their training, experience and wisdom, as well as with the practical magic of poetry therapy.

Now the National Association for Poetry Therapy offers this collection as a resource to the global community. I am proud of the proactive stand this collection represents, and I am humbled by its healing potential. To everyone who offered poems, and to the publishing companies that extended royalty-free permission to reprint previously published works, I extend my sincere appreciation.

May this inspired collection speak to you in a clear voice about the universal experience of loss, and the universal capacity of poetry to offer strength and solace as we find our way through to hope and healing.

Kathleen Adams
Denver, Colorado

INTRODUCTION:
SEASONS OF THE HEART

When tragedy strikes, poetry happens.

Whether the tragedy is the loss of a loved one, a cataclysmic natural disaster, the end of a meaningful relationship or an assault on safety and peace of mind, our emotions around tragic events are so strong that they command our attention. As we focus on our emotions, the desire and need to express them grows. That's when poetry happens.

We each saw this in the cultural phenomenon of September 11, 2001. Out of the devastation, shock, horror and despair came an unprecedented flow of poetry. Written on notebook paper, napkins, envelopes; in e-mails, newsletters, magazines; posted on street corners, subway stations, makeshift memorials. Poetry was a first response to this tragedy and it appeared in such volume and with such persistence that it was impossible not to notice.

As poetry therapists, we believe in the power of poetry to help people cope with tragic events. This anthology was created in order to share a collection of poems in which a vast range of responses to tragic events are examined and expressed, from horror and disbelief, through confrontation and acceptance, to healing and growth.

The process through which poetry leads to healing is quite simple, yet undeniably profound. By writing about our experiences and feelings, or sharing the experiences and feelings of another as expressed in a poem, we gain a better understanding of them. This is because honest expression opens the door to insight, clarity and understanding. The poet's search for the words that best express experience and feeling is a process of sifting, sorting, selecting, choosing. Rhythm and sound add texture and nuance to the search. Whether we are the poet/writer or the reader/listener, we participate in a process of honest self-expression, where we carefully probe feelings and experiences and place them into the shared context of language. Both writer and receiver can then experience the relief of deepened understanding and, often, a reduction of anxiety as vague fears and concerns are made clear.

However healing it may be to write an original poem or read or hear the honest writing of another, there is an additional dimension of healing available when these activities are undertaken in community. When we share poems such as those found in this collection with others, we gain further understanding from exploring our reactions in thoughtful discussion. Writing, sharing and discussing our own poems, stories and journal entries can add yet another layer of richness. The activities offered in the back of the book for reading and discussing poetry, and the writing suggestions provided for each poem, may be useful for getting things started.

We hope that these poems will provide comfort, permission and safety to give your own sorrow words—to place carefully into language the thoughts and feelings that are among the most difficult, overwhelming and complex in the human experience—the seasons of the heart.

Karen vanMeenen
Rochester, New York

Charles Rossiter
Chicago, Illinois

POEMS:
AUTUMN

AUTUMN

The leaves are falling, falling as if from far up,
as if orchards were dying high in space.
Each leaf falls as if it were motioning "no."

And tonight the heavy earth is falling
away from all the stars in the loneliness.

We're all falling. This hand here is falling.
And look at the other one. . . . It's in them all.

And yet there is Someone, whose hands
infinitely calm, hold up all this falling.

Rainer Maria Rilke
translated Robert Bly

HOW BAD NEWS COMES

A telephone is ringing
like an emergency
in a room down the hall,
I think of the one
to whom bad news
is coming. At the market,
she's touching fruit,
or driving home,
strumming her fingers
on the steering wheel.
This is the way life
insists on itself, his scent
still on her as she reaches
for the phone, happy
to catch it in mid-ring,
coming through
the door, her keys
still dangling in the lock.
Unclipping an earring
as she leans in to hear
the voice on the other end
saying, I've got some
bad news, feeling
in that long second
before the words come
the difference between
the way it was
and the way
it will be, that moment
before the groceries
fall to the floor.

Debra Marquart

ASH TUESDAY

Each year as Lent begins,
ashes on our foreheads
give us stark reminder
of our fragile state;
yet we were not prepared for
fathers, friends, firefighters,
neighbors to be thrust
one sunny New York morning
into a crematorium.
I want to scoop that ash
into holy family urns
for display on mantles
spread across this world
as a reminder of
how perishable we are,
what seeds of hate can grow,
how bound we are together,
what love must overcome.
Let this terrible Tuesday
begin a worldwide Lent
of prayer, self-examination,
repentance and renewed
heart determination
to shine forth light and serve
a Lord of life and love,
until from earth's great ash heap
every body rises.

Ann Grizzle

CASTE

The boat called your hand floats
over a paper lake
restocked you are
in your fishing hat you
must not fish for the meaningful
do not fish to be full
catch a glimpse and release
flashfisher   fast-caster   hauler of hope
Others waste their mornings
ironing their shirts
cleaning last night's beanfield off their shoes

Spend no time grooming the body if
there's a glimpse to be groomed   go to work naked
hair like a weed patch   feet a fleet of plows
Blessed are those who skip breakfast to write
and work hungry. Forge a new myth growling
for something we can sink our teeth in

Take on the mob or the president
swing your doors wide and place your
laugherSelf framed in the screen
door for all the drive-by shooters
Write where the music is first one thing
and then another. Put your distracting
flag away. When they ask why you do
anything you do, tell them it is because of
the airplanes that flew. It is their job to
tell you what you mean. Yours to make us
uncomfortable.
Lie on the floor in a room with
rice-paper windows. Look through

parchment doubt. Everything reported
and that you see for yourself—
each incident—is a list of reasons you were spared.
Every terror has its counterJoy you were
born to invent.

Jennifer Bosveld

FALLING

This morning I lost my footing,
slid down stairs
on my back,
no bone broken.
Just a wrist burn
and single spot of blood
where my skin broke open.

Two evenings ago
Shira slipped bareback
from her horse
and hit her head.
She lost her time and place,
all memory of the ride.
From the ER home I prayed
and woke her each two hours
as she lay beside me,
grown-up baby, in the bed.

All week the dust
From New York City
and Washington and Pittsburgh
has seeped through windows
and doors, has blown
over the streets, even here
in quiet New Hampshire.
I trip over rubble in the grocery,
turn to every TV
making sure it's real.

All week we've been falling,
you and I, friend,
holding hands across the miles.
Sending poems and prayers
to find the ground
and the wellsprings,
giving blood, offering money,
speaking when we
don't know how to speak.
Loving as hard as we can.

Lisa Friedlander

I lost a member of my family.
A grandfather, a grandmother,
a sister, son and brother.
I lost my father, my mother,
my English cousin, my Japanese daughter.
I lost a member of my family,
my Israeli every man,
my American every woman,
my family,
extended, nuclear and
everything is immediate.
I have veiled my mirrors,
removed my leather shoes,
said Kaddish nearly six thousand times
said Kaddish six million times
I have lost a member of my family
I will sit Shiva seven days
I will grieve forever.

Jerri Chaplin

MUSLIM PRAYER FOR PEACE

In the name of Allah,
the beneficent, the merciful.
Praise be to the Lord of the
Universe who has created us and
made us into tribes and nations
That we may know each other, not that
we may despise each other.
If the enemy incline towards peace, do
thou also incline towards peace, and
trust God, for the Lord is the one that
heareth and knoweth all things.
And the servants of God,
Most gracious are those who walk on
the Earth in humility, and when we
address them, we say "PEACE."

Poems:
Winter

THE DEAD

The dead are always looking down on us, they say,
while we are putting on our shoes or making a sandwich,
they are looking down through the glass-bottom boats
    of heaven
as they row themselves slowly through eternity.

They watch the tops of our heads moving below on earth,
and when we lie down in a field or on a couch,
drugged perhaps by the hum of a warm afternoon,
they think we are looking back at them,

which makes them lift their oars and fall silent
and wait, like parents, for us to close our eyes.

Billy Collins

VEILS

In school children are writing themselves down
on paper, poems full of hopes, loves, dreams.
Somewhere in the middle of a perfect horseback ride
or friendly game, today they fall, go inside a black hole
with no sides. Next thing, they write they are in heaven
with silver wings, parents there too in a whole world.
And we wonder if those who terrify us
welcome death for a similar reason. Allah Allah.

I walk on the beach with a friend on a mute afternoon,
two new widows floating in an unsure line
covered head to foot in veils of fleece
against the chill of fog and news, our guilt—
you can never do enough for death.
The world stands on one leg barely breathing.

It is good to name the birds as they return
with the receding tide, the newly arrived plover
with its black eye, a mass of sandpipers rejoicing
the shore. And the wimbrels, bless them, the willits
and curlews whose names need to be remembered too,
and the children's: Will, Amber, Magdalena, Nivan.
Can we bring down heaven, plant it here where they live?
Allah Allah. Such thick veils.

Perie Longo

DADDY, WHAT COLOR IS THUNDER?

for Erika 5/4/70 - 8/7/89

And you were there, in the wrong place
at the wrong time, innocent, midday,
on a familiar two lane road and probably
singing along with the radio

Erika, I see you everywhere, in the mirror,
my eyes are your eyes, my body—
the body you once had, now ashes
in the sea. Be still, daughter
the tides will take you

You will know the color of thunder.

Charles Rossiter

THE THING IS

to love life, to love it even
when you have no stomach for it
and everything you've held dear
crumbles like burnt paper in your hands,
your throat filled with the silt of it.
When grief sits with you, its tropical heat
thickening the air, heavy as water
more fit for gills than lungs;
When grief weights you like your own flesh
only more of it, an obesity of grief.
you think, *how can a body withstand this?*
Then you hold life like a face
between your palms, a plain face,
no charming smile, no violet eyes,
and you say, yes, I will take you
I will love you, again.

Ellen Bass

TIDE

If I don't catch it
right now, the look of the bay
at the lowest tide,
with the sun stamping on it,
the uncovered sand like clay,

if I let it go
for some more important thing,
or just look away
for a bit, meaning to note it
when I've first done something else,

only my mind's eye
will be left to remember,
when the tide has turned,
how the whole bay looked
like a great shell lying there

all blue, brown, silver
and how I needed to shape
something I could hold
and keep, maybe, from those few
moments before it all changed.

Susan Donnelly

WHEN YOU LEAVE US

When you move wordlessly
from one life into another,
you will bring all of us
who have ever declared our love,
with our hearts, or with our mouths.
We walk with you arm in arm,
and instead of leaving us at the gate,
you find we all have to enter with you.
We all see a new maple, a bush on fire,
A tiny sparrow perched on a flat rock.

You cannot leave us and we
cannot leave you.

Though you have made your entrance
into a new home,
our old homes are full of the things
you loved. You live on mantles,
in journals, on a recipe card
splattered with sugar cookie dough.

When night comes, we are certain
you hear our voices,
low and full on brick patios,
ice cubes swirling in our paper cups.

Nothing is nearer than love itself,
even when this life has carefully tucked you in,
closed your bedroom window,
whispered its soft goodnight.

We are only steps away from you,
through the clear glass,
on the other side of the pane.
If we listen carefully,
underneath the crickets and the murmur of twilight,
we will still hear you breathing,
as steady
as the slow dance that begins among us,
underneath the patient stars.

Joy Sawyer

WHILE WATCHING A VIDEO OF THE DALAI LAMA

for my husband

Everything I see or hear is about him
since he has been gone,
this morning the Dalai Lama
who says there is so much suffering
in the world he can't do much.

With his monks he sifts colored sand
into an intricate design for peace,
then sweeps it away. They collect
the remains in a small jar, sprinkle a little
on top of their heads for tranquillity.

While I held my husband in my hands
as ash, like finest sand,
all the hard edges of us disappeared
with the smoke. I rubbed him on my skin

then flew him off to light.

Such tragedy! how it takes death
to put everything in its right place,
how it takes death to make a life perfect.

Perie Longo

FOR MY YOUNG FRIENDS WHO ARE AFRAID

There is a country to cross you will
find in the corner of your eye, in
the quick slip of your foot—air far
down, a snap that might have caught.
And maybe for you, for me, a high, passing
voice that finds its way by being
afraid. That country is there, for us,
carried as it is crossed. What you fear
will not go away: it will take you into
yourself and bless you and keep you.
That's the world, and we all live there.

William Stafford

OBJIBWAY PRAYER

Grandfather,
Look at our brokenness.

We know that in all creation
Only the human family
Has strayed from the Sacred Way.

We know that we are the ones
Who are divided,
And we are the ones
Who must come back together
To walk the Sacred Way.

Grandfather,
Sacred One,
Teach us love, compassion, and honor
That we may heal the earth
And heal each other.

POEMS:
SPRING

HOPI PRAYER

Hold on to what is good
even if it's a handful of earth.
Hold on to what you believe
even if it's a tree that stands by itself.
Hold on to what you must do
even if it's a long way from here.
Hold on to your life
even if it's easier to let go.
Hold on to my hand
even when I've gone away from you.

HOPE IT'S TRUE

I have a small grain of hope—
One small crystal that gleams
Clear colors out of transparency.

I need more.

I break off a fragment
To send you.
Please take
This grain of hope
So mine won't shrink.

Please share your fragment
So that yours will grow.

Only so, by division,
Will hope increase,

Like a clump of irises which will cease to flower
Unless you distribute
The clustered roots, unlikely source—
Clumsy and earth-covered—
Of grace.

Denise Levertov

AIRPLANES OF THE HEART

The little airplanes of the heart
with their brave little propellers
What can they do
against the winds of darkness
even as butterflies are beaten back
by hurricanes
yet do not die
They lie in wait wherever
they can hide and hang
their fine wings folded
and when the killer-wind dies
they flutter forth again
into the new-blown light
live as leaves

Lawrence Ferlinghetti

29

PAKISTAN WITH OPEN ARMS

Tonight in Karachi, a man drapes
jasmine garlands over his wrist
and looks both ways.
It is the hour of the walk,
when men and women come slowly forth
from houses, kitchens,
their stride growing long and musical,
sky finally softening its grip.
Whatever they talked about in the day
stands back to let them pass.

In some languages, a voice asking
a question goes up at the end
and an answer slopes toward the sea.
Maybe now the turtles are stepping
from their nests at the beach,
the huge shrine of their eggs behind them.
Maybe the fabulous painted buses
are cooling their engines at the lot.

How could I have seen, twenty years ago,
a night when a string of fragrant flowers
would be all that I desired?
In the peaked shadow of his house
a man reads a map on which deserts
and mountains are different colors.
Each province has its own woven rugs
and speckled red hats.
He wishes to walk in a hundred villages
where people he will never meet are walking.

Into my arms I gather the quiet avenue,
the patience of curbs.
A family relaxes on a sweep of public grass.
Their shirts are cotton and silk.
They visit quietly as the moon comes speaking
its simple round name.
I gather them into me, saying,
This is the thunderous city.
This is the person who once was afraid.

Naomi Shihab Nye

HOPE

Hope
is the belief
that one hand
reaching to another
can eventually
touch the moon,
allowing the light
to guide us
through the night.

Nicholas Mazza

YES

It could happen any time, tornado,
earthquake, Armageddon. It could happen.
Or sunshine, love, salvation.

It could you know. That's why we wake
and look out—no guarantees
in this life.

But some bonuses, like morning,
like right now, like noon,
like evening.

William Stafford

THE ROAD

The road to my new home
climbs steeply up a hill called Beacon:
romantic name, evoking
shelter, comfort, light
in the dark, relief in the hearts
of travelers lost at sea.

My road to Beacon Hill
has been so steep, began
in pain so deep, my soul
awash in loss, screams
and pleas silenced
in anesthesia, waking
to the unbearable.

And going on: inexplicably
sleeping and waking
each day to the unbearable,
every day still alive,
every day my son still dead.

People speak of courage, ask
"how do you do it?" No answer but
"I just keep waking up."
And yet in some deep resilient
fiber-nerve of being I know:
Something chooses.

From Beacon Hill I see
lakewater to the east,
saltwater to the west,
the mountains beyond.

Each day the sun lifts
through rose-mauve mist
hangs high then sinks
to smoldering purple and gold
pushing against the dark.
And every day I too rise,
and through survivor's eyes
I look, and see,
and tell him.

Alma Maria Rolfs

ELEGY TO THE WOUNDED WORLD

Impossible here to believe that the world is so wounded,
    so many
already dead, so many more to die. At the retreat house,
    we can believe,

at least for this weekend, that the world is not imploding,
    forget the images
of people trying to run from war, the father holding his
    son's hand and walking

beside his cart with wooden wheels, his long, feet
    churning dust or the image of a
father teaching his 5 year old son how to shoot a gun. The
    announcer's voice says

in Afghanistan. The children are taught to use guns and
    often are conscripted into
the army before they reach puberty. The evergreens sit
    plump as matrons outside

the window, the sun illuminating the Convent's white-
    washed walls. The air
is full of that deep earthy smell: fallen leaves, moss. The
    cycle of life and death,

clear here for the first time since we saw the towers fall.
    How we believed in our own
invincible safety: our blessed lives as Americans, our
    ability to go anywhere and not be

afraid. Now we must carry the wounded world like a
    dying child in our arms forever.

Maria Mazziotti Gillan

ELBOWS

The sacred quality
of arms, particularly
elbows that make
each of us working class,
put us here for a purpose.
Look at elbows and
what they say:
elbow your way
into the passive crowd
to do what is needed,
give it your elbow grease—
this is enough.
Elbows, no one can
possess them because
they can disappear and
you move them
into action by choice.
And that choice
is prayer in action.
The deepest current of love
is not found in the heart.
That is the certain spring,
the natural ease, the flow
from the mountaintop.
The greatest current of love
rushes forward in the choice
to make a cradle of the body.

John Fox

Hold It

Hold it:

Cat footprints across a table,
Print them
As deeply as a headache.

Magpies arguing over figs,
Listen until
Your ears crack.

Mosquito aimed for your wrist,
Anticipate the prick
Long after she's fed.

Sliced cantaloupe,
Inhale
Until the scent stops
Your breath.

Lover's kiss,
Taste the sweet salt,
Your tongue remembers
Nothing else.

Hold it:

An overflow of bees in the lavender.

Angry voices next door.

Your shoe sucked off by mud.

Shattering glass.
Bats harvesting insects at twilight.

Your mouth ready for garlic, tomatoes, olive oil, capers.

A shoe and a torn shirt in the alley.

A siren.

Hold it:

That ordinariness,
Hold,
as it
Hurts, cracks, caresses, saves
us.

Kathi Brown-Favrot

SIOUX PRAYER

Our Father the Sky, hear us and make us bold.
O Our Mother the Earth, hear us and give us support.
O Spirit of the East, send us your wisdom.
O Spirit of the South, may we walk your path of life.
O Spirit of the West, may we always be ready for the
        long journey.
O Spirit of the North, purify us with your cleansing winds.

NEW BONES

we will wear
new bones again
these rainy days,
break out through
another mouth
into sun and honey time.
worlds buzz over us like bees
we be splendid in new bones.
other people think they know
how long life is
how strong life is
we know.

Lucille Clifton

RESOURCES

USING POETRY FOR GROWTH AND HEALING: A BRIEF GUIDE FOR INDIVIDUALS AND HELPING PROFESSIONALS

A poem can be a source of joy, a source of comfort, a source of solace, as well as a work of art. In this collection we have brought together a wide range of poems that speak to issues all of us face in uncertain times when grief robs us of peace of mind and heart.

Poetry can be an important source of growth and healing. Reading poems in which our own feelings are expressed and reflected upon helps us to feel less alone. When we are able to read about experiences similar to our own in poems, we know that others have gone through what we are going through. We are validated in our experience and existence.

For years, poetry therapists have worked to develop ways to enhance the power of poems for personal growth and healing. Our goal is to share some of those pathways here so that your experience of the poems in this book will be more powerful and helpful.

The key to growth is understanding. The key to successful grieving is acceptance. The activities suggested here will help you to delve more deeply into your own feelings and experiences in order to increase personal understanding and acceptance. In doing these activities, there is no absolute right or wrong. There is only the doing, and in the doing there is growth.

The first thing to know about writing for self-expression is that there are no rules beyond the effort to be honest. With this kind of writing you are the expert. What you think, believe and feel are your thoughts, beliefs and feelings. You are the ultimate expert. How you write for self-expression is also completely up to you. No editor, teacher or other authority will critique how you write about yourself. If you want to write long run-on sentences, feel free. If it pleases you to write one word on each line, do it. If you want to mix poetry and prose, go ahead. If you're at a computer and want to use unusual fonts that feel right according to what you want to say, go for it. The point is to look inside and to write what you find there.

The suggested activities are geared for response to individual poems. You can begin anywhere. As some poems in the collection will speak to you more strongly, it is probably best to start with those. As you proceed, feel free to modify the activities in any way that feels useful to you. Basically, anything you do that enhances your exploration of personal issues and feelings can help lead you to new understandings and greater feelings of wholeness.

At the most basic level, there are three things you can do to respond to poetry: Read it, talk about it and write your own poems or journal entries in response to it. Use these guidelines to help you take one or more of these three steps.

READING POEMS FOR PERSONAL GROWTH

Try reading the poem several different ways. Start with reading it to yourself silently. Then read it again, more slowly. Pause at the end of each line. Go back and re-read lines or phrases that have particular impact. Then read it out loud, even if it is a whisper. See how the poem changes when it is given voice and breath.

If a poem is particularly rich or has significant impact for you, memorize it. Say it to yourself over and over. Write it in your own handwriting, or type it into a computer. Carry copies of the poem with you. Refer to it often. Let its rhythm and presence accompany you throughout the day. There may be a line, a phrase, that repeats itself over and over inside your head. Allow this line or phrase to be a companion, and be curious about it. Let it guide you to new understanding. This process can be subtle; it is not unusual for it to take weeks, months or even years to fully comprehend what the poem is teaching you.

DISCUSSING POEMS FOR PERSONAL GROWTH

The typical format used by poetry therapists to explore personal issues through poetry in groups is as follows:

1. Distribute copies of the poem. Be sure to include the poet's name and the source from which it came.

2. Have someone from the group read the poem aloud. For longer poems, participants may want to read a few lines at a time and pass it around the group so that several voices are heard.

3. Read the poem aloud a second time. If there is a group leader or facilitator, that person may want to read the poem the second time. Or another participant may read it, or the group may read it collectively again, starting with a different reader so that each person reads different lines than the first time through.

4. Invite comments with the clear indication that anything goes. This means that there are no right or wrong answers. In this context, emphasis on poetics—the form the poem takes, the skill of the poet—is not encouraged. The point of this kind of discussion is to explore the ideas expressed in the poem and reflect upon how these ideas may or may not be personally meaningful.

47

5. Sometimes it helps get the discussion going if the group leader, or a group member, poses the question, "Are there any lines, phrases, images that especially speak to you? Say them out loud." When everyone has had a chance to respond, the group leader can follow up with process questions, such as, "What does this poem say to you?" or "How does this poem reflect or address something in your life experience?"

WRITING FOR PERSONAL GROWTH

For this kind of writing, you don't need to be a poet. You don't even need to frame your writing in the shape of a poem. Write paragraphs or lists if that feels good to you. The important thing is to express your own honest thoughts and feelings. Below are possible ways to use individual poems in this collection as springboards to your own exploration of issues. These suggestions are simply to get you started. The best suggestion for writing in response to a poem is to follow your pen wherever it leads you. If, having started, your writing takes off in a completely different direction, then follow along with curiosity and let it evolve spontaneously.

If writing is undertaken in community, it is important to let the group know that sharing what has been written is *always* optional. It is the facilitator's or group leader's responsibility to give permission to *not* share. Poetry therapists usually suggest that sharing can also consist of speaking about the process of writing, or summarizing any insight or learning from what has been written.

Likewise, it is important to emphasize that group discussion will be centered on the feelings and process conveyed in the writing rather than on subjective opinions about the writing itself. The point is never to write "well," although surprisingly "good" writing often surfaces when permission is given to simply write without expectations.

Autumn, Rainer Maria Rilke, translated by Robert Bly (p. 3)
Just as the seasons change, death comes as a part of life. The universal loneliness of loss is tempered in this poem by the suggestion that there is a Someone whose quiet presence is available to soothe us. Does faith play a role in your acceptance of what life brings you? In what ways?

How Bad News Comes, Debra Marquart (p. 4)
Part of the grieving process involves reliving its individual moments of trauma. Writing helps provide a container for this natural and necessary experience. Write a poem about how bad news came to you.

Ash Tuesday, Ann Grizzle (p. 5)
We are all vunerable, but still we carry on. What else can we do? This poem contemplates our human frailty, a subject that can be discussed with friends or loved ones, or written about in a poem. If you observe Lent, write about a personal experience of the Lenten season that had particular meaning. Or write about a time when you experienced personal sacrifice, your own or another's.

Caste, Jennifer Bosveld (p. 6)
Take a wild stream-of-consciousness ride in which you let yourself write whatever comes, without censoring or editing. Or try this writing activity that is often used in poetry therapy workshops or sessions: Select seven words from this poem and use them in a poem of your own. If you'd rather have a more random spark to your creativity, use these seven words: boat; airplane; fish; music; terror; blessed; myth.

Falling, Lisa Friedlander (p. 8)
How do you stay grounded when everything around you is falling apart? Where do you reach for comfort and sustenance? Reflect on the ways you do or do not "love as hard as (you) can" when you experience disaster, small or large.

Untitled, Jerri Chaplin (p. 10) *Certified Poetry Therapist*
This is a list poem in which the poet catalogs people she has lost. A list poem can repeat any phrase to create a chant-like incantation. Try writing your own list poem using the phrase "I feel this way because . . . " or "I lost . . ." It isn't necessary that each line begin with the repeated phrase.

Muslim Prayer for Peace (p. 11)
The peace prayers of the major world religions speak in a universal voice. Write your own prayer for peace, drawing from as many wisdom traditions as you can.

The Dead, Billy Collins (p. 15)
Many cultures have elaborate stories about what happens after death. This poem provides a contemporary story of how the dead relate to us. Reflect on someone you love who has died. Imagine that person watching you. What does he or she notice? What is she or he feeling? Try writing a poem in the voice of the one who has died.

Veils, Perie Longo (p. 16) *Registered Poetry Therapist*
This poem juxtaposes the collective trauma of world events with the very individualized act of naming. When circumstances become overwhelming, when "you can never do enough for death," how can you make it manageable again? What can you name or individualize to draw aside the veils and acknowledge the life that remains?

Daddy, What Color is Thunder?, Charles Rossiter
(p. 17) *Certified Poetry Therapist*
Confronting head-on the death of a loved one is never easy, but it is a powerful aid in the grieving process. In this poem, the poet focuses on details of a deceased daughter. To write this kind of poem, you need to get a clear mental image of the person you are writing about. It may help to look at pictures in the family album or watch a family video. Recall in your mind how the person moved and looked and talked. Then, put it down on paper.

The Thing Is, Ellen Bass (p. 18)
This poem suggests that, even when it is hardest, we can love and appreciate life. Reflect on your own willingness to "hold life like a face between your palms" when it is the most difficult. When you are most loving of life, what do you do? When you are the most depressed or grief-stricken, how do you cope? Make a list, or a list poem, that includes your coping strategies and your life-affirming activities. How many of these things do you do on a regular basis? How many more could you do? This is a good writing activity to do with others, comparing and discussing responses.

Tide, Susan Donnelly (p. 19)
The poet needs something to hold and keep. Find an object you have held and kept to help you hold onto an experience. Use the object as stimulus for writing. What strength or solace did you derive from this object? It's interesting to do this with a group of people who can show their objects while they share their writing or talk about the process of writing it.

When You Leave Us, Joy Sawyer (p. 20) *Certified Poetry Therapist*
Death does not end relationships. Relationships have their own life cycle. This poem points out the ongoing relationship we have with those who have died or moved on. Try writing your own poem about all the ways in which one who has left is still present in your ongoing life.

While Watching a Video of the Dalai Lama, Perie Longo (p. 22) *Registered Poetry Therapist*
The presence of those we love lives after them. In this poem, everything is about the one who is missed. Consider the many places where you still see a loved one who has passed away. Write a poem about those places or merely list them and read the list aloud. At another level, the poet speaks of the way "hard edges disappeared" with death. How did your relationship with your loved one change through death?

For My Young Friends Who Are Afraid, William Stafford (p. 23)
This poem teaches us that fear is not only normal and natural, but a teacher and even a blessing. How has fear been a teacher for you? How has fear blessed you? Write about a time when you leaned into fear, when you crossed the border into a new land.

Objibway Prayer (p. 24)
What do you see when you "look at (y)our brokenness"? See your own brokenness with loving, compassionate eyes. Invoke the presence of a benevolent wisdom figure and honestly, heartfully release to it the places where you are divided. Write a prayer poem or an unsent letter to this wisdom figure.

Hopi Prayer (p. 27)
To what do you hold on when all looks bleak and desolate? Write a poem in which you alternate the lines "Hold on to . . ." and "even if . . ."

Hope It's True, Denise Levertov (p. 28)
This poem deals with the paradox of creating more by giving away. What in your life increases as you release it? How easy or difficult is it for you to trust this? You may also want to write your own poem on the topic of hope.

Airplanes of the Heart, Lawrence Ferlinghetti (p. 29)
This poem explores themes of tenacity and the strength of the life force. What do you do when the hurricane winds blow? How do you hang on until it's safe to come out? Write and discuss.

Pakistan With Open Arms, Naomi Shihab Nye (p. 30)
It is often difficult to know and understand another person—to "walk a mile in their moccasins," as the Native American proverb suggests. Fully entering into their world and perceiving life through their eyes allows us to "gather" them into us and promotes unity and understanding. Write a journal entry or poem in the voice of another you seek to understand. Or see if you can enter into his/her world and write about what you observe.

Hope, Nicholas Mazza (p. 32) *Registered Poetry Therapist*
A metaphor is something in the tangible world that stands in for something intangible. This short poem, with only a few words on each line, relies on metaphor. Read it through several times and get a clear picture of the visual image it suggests. Free-write for five or ten minutes on the visual images suggested by an intangible quality such as hope, faith, trust, belief. Then write a small metaphor poem.

Yes, William Stafford (p. 33)
We have each had the experience of our lives changing forever in a moment—an accident, a sudden death, the terrorist attacks of September 11. This brief poem helps us contain the fear of uncertainty and balance it with hope. The poet points us toward present-centeredness and appreciation of the "now" moment. What is your "now" moment? What can you find to appreciate within it? Write a poem of praise for this exact moment, right now.

The Road, Alma Maria Rolfs (p. 34) *Registered Poetry Therapist*
The poet considers the long road she has traveled following tragedy to get where she is today. Recalling outcomes of past experiences reminds us that we have the strength to overcome current tragedies. Think of a past dark time in your life and consider the road you have traveled from that time until now. Write about your travels.

Elegy to the Wounded World, Maria Mazziotti Gillan (p. 36)
The juxtaposition of two opposite realities—the trauma of September 11 and the contemplative peace behind cloistered walls—are contained in simple two-line stanzas. When you reach deeply within to your own place of peace, what do you offer to the wounded places in you? Try writing your own elegy to the wounded world, or to your wounded self. Experiment with the form of two-line stanzas to capture and hold the dichotomy.

Elbows, John Fox (p. 37) *Certified Poetry Therapist*
This poem takes a mundane body part and infuses it with meaning. Select a particular body part, or something in your everyday world that seems mundane, and use it as a subject for a poem. Notice how the poet emphasizes the

sacred. See if you can use your poem or writing to find the sacred within the ordinary.

Hold It, Kathi Brown-Favrot (p. 38)

This poem lists everyday things to be savored. Its beauty lies in its specificity. Create your own poem list of everyday experiences that give your life added meaning. Be as detailed and specific as you can. Put a copy of your poem on your refrigerator or bathroom mirror where you will be sure to see it every day.

Sioux Prayer (p. 40)

Nature teaches us that everything in the human world, no matter how devastating or traumatizing, can be placed in the larger context of the natural world. Write a poem or a prayer to the earth, focusing on the ways you draw strength and comfort from nature.

new bones, Lucille Clifton (p. 41)

After the long cold winter of grieving, the stage of acceptance eventually comes and we "wear new bones again." What do you anticipate on the other side of grief and loss? What will your "sun and honey" time look like? Try a poem with a first line of, "My sun and honey time . . ." How has living through difficulty helped you grow "new bones"? What do you "know" about life and yourself now that you didn't know before?

Kathleen Adams
Charles Rossiter
Karen vanMeenen

WHAT IS POETRY THERAPY?

Poetry therapy utilizes poetry, journals and literature for healing and personal growth. Through the processes of reading and writing poetry, as well as sharing with others, it is possible to access feelings, motivations, memories and unconscious desires and drives.

Poetry therapists work in mental health, medical, geriatric, therapeutic, educational, religious and community settings. Poetry therapy, journal therapy and bibliotherapy—all of which are collectively referred to as "poetry therapy"—have a broad range of applications with people of all ages and abilities. It is successfully used with people across the life span, in nearly every life circumstance, for physical, mental, emotional and spiritual healing and wellness.

Poetry therapists can be found globally, with practitioners throughout the United States and in Israel, Japan, India, Canada, European countries, South American countries, South Africa and other nations. Practitioners include psychiatrists, psychologists, social workers, physicians, nurses, mental health counselors, addictions counselors, pastoral counselors, educators, librarians, poets in the schools and community-based art programs, community activists, clergy, spiritual directors, occupational therapists, recreational therapists, prison workers, community volunteers, poets, writers and more.

Certification to become a Certified Poetry Therapist (CPT) or Registered Poetry Therapist (RPT) is available through the National Federation for Biblio/Poetry Therapy. CPTs work at the community level, and it is not necessary to be a psychotherapist or helping professional, although a Bachelor's degree is required. RPTs work both at the community level and clinically. An advanced degree or licensure in psychology, counseling, psychiatry or a related field is required for the RPT. The rigorous training program required for the CPT (440 hours) or the RPT (975 hours) is guided by an approved Mentor/Supervisor. Graduate degree programs are available in poetry therapy, therapeutic writing and transformative language arts at a growing number of colleges and universities.

You may request information at www.poetrytherapy.org/training/training.htm or by ordering the CPT/RPT Guidebook for $25 plus $5 shipping and handling from sdietz@assoc-mgmt.com or by calling (866) 844-NAPT.

NATIONAL ASSOCIATION FOR
POETRY THERAPY (NAPT)

NAPT is an energetic, worldwide community of people who share a love for the use of language arts in healing and growth. Members represent a wide range of professional experience, schools of therapy, educational affiliations, artistic disciplines and other fields of training in both mental and physical health. In addition to its professional membership, NAPT welcomes all persons who are interested in the power of the healing word.

Membership in the Association offers services such as a quarterly newsletter, the quarterly academic *Journal of Poetry Therapy*, educational seminars with the master teachers in the field, training opportunities, regional and national conferences, collegial support and informal networking opportunities.

THE NAPT FOUNDATION

The NAPT Foundation is a 501(c)(3) nonprofit educational foundation that supports NAPT and the field of poetry therapy. The ongoing work of the Foundation includes scholarship opportunities and grants for poetry therapists and those in training; seed money grants to bring poetry therapy to audiences and populations that would not otherwise have access; and broadening awareness of poetry therapy through outreach programs.

All donations to the NAPT Foundation are tax-deductible. 100% of funds collected are allocated for charitable and educational use.

The funding for this book is provided through a grant from the NAPT Foundation.

FOR ADDITIONAL COPIES OF THIS BOOK . . .

• There is no charge for the books. They are offered free to individuals, helping professionals and others who might benefit from their use. Postage costs (U.S.) are $3.00 for each book ($5 each for international postage, payable in U.S. funds only), mailed in the form of a check or money order made out to NAPT Foundation, 525 SW 5th St., Suite A, Des Moines, IA 50309-4501.

• Postage costs may also be paid through the website, www.poetrytherapy.org/foundation.htm, using a Mastercard/Visa.

To make a donation to the NAPT Foundation . . .

• Your donation to the NAPT Foundation helps keep this book in print and available to all who can use it. All donations are tax-deductible.

• Donations may be made at the website, www. poetrytherapy.org/foundation.htm

To find a poetry therapist in your area . . .

• See www.poetrytherapy.org/training.directory.htm

To arrange a poetry therapy intern for your practice, organization or agency . . .

• See www.poetrytherapy.org/training/mentor_supervisors. htm. Note that many poetry therapists train through distance learning, so many more geographic areas are represented than appear on the mentor/supervisor list.

For a comprehensive folder describing applications of poetry therapy for medical and mental illness and wellness . . .

• Request the "Integrative Medicine" folder by calling (866) 844-NAPT or e-mailing sdietz@assoc-mgmt.com.

To become a poetry therapist . . .

• See www.poetrytherapy.org/training/training.htm

• Order the CPT/RPT Training Guide ($25 plus $5 shipping and handling) at the website or by calling (866) 844-NAPT

To join the National Association for Poetry Therapy . . .

• Call (866) 844-NAPT or e-mail sdietz@assoc-mgmt.com

• Join online at www.poetrytherapy.org/members/ membership.htm

For more information about NAPT . . .

• Visit our website at www.poetrytherapy.org

ACKNOWLEDGMENTS

The editors have made every effort to locate the copyright holders for all works contained herein, and credit those individuals and sources below for permission to reproduce material in this book. Any errors are unintentional and we regret any oversights. The editors welcome notification of any incomplete information for correction in future editions.

Ellen Bass: "The Thing Is" from *Mules Of Love* by Ellen Bass, BOA Editions, Rochester, NY, 2002. © 1998 by Ellen Bass. Reprinted by permission of the author.

Robert Bly, trans.,: "Autumn" by Rainer Maria Rilke from *Selected Poems of Rainer Maria Rilke*, HarperCollins, New York, 1981. © 1981 by Robert Bly. Reprinted by permission of Robert Bly.

Lucille Clifton: "new bones" © 1997 by Lucille Clifton. Reprinted from *Good Woman: Poems and a Memoir, 1969-1980* by Lucille Clifton by permission of BOA Editions, Ltd.

Billy Collins: "The Dead" from *Questions About Angels* by Billy Collins © 1991. Reprinted by permission of the University of Pittsburgh Press.

Susan Donnelly: "Tide" from *Transition*, Iris Press, Oak Ridge, TN, 2001. © 2001 by Susan Donnelly. Reprinted by permission of the author.

Lawrence Ferlinghetti: "Airplanes of the Heart" was first published as "Sandinista Avioncito" in *City Lights Review*, 1989. It also appears in *These are My Rivers: New and Selected Poems, 1955-1993*, New Directions, New York, © 1993 by Lawrence Ferlinghetti. Reprinted by permission of the author.

Denise Levertov: "Hope It's True" from *Poems 1968-1972*, © 1972 by Denise Levertov. Reprinted by permission of New Directions Publishing Corp., New York.

61

GIVING SORROW WORDS:

POEMS OF STRENGTH AND SOLACE

EDITED BY KAREN vanMEENEN
AND CHARLES ROSSITER
WITH KATHLEEN ADAMS

NATIONAL ASSOCIATION FOR
POETRY THERAPY
FOUNDATION

DES MOINES, IOWA

National Association for Poetry Therapy Foundation

525 SW 5th St., Suite A

Des Moines, IA 50309-4501

tel: (866) 844-NAPT

www.poetrytherapy.org

Text designed by Karen vanMeenen

Cover designed by Hal Aqua

Fourth printing

ISBN 0-9676552-3-4

Printed in the United States of America

ABOUT THE EDITORS

Karen vanMeenen, MA, CPT is a Board Member of NAPT, where she serves as Editor of the quarterly publication *The Museletter* and Chair of the Publications Committee. She has a Master of Arts degree in Transformative Language Arts from Vermont College and is a Certified Poetry Therapist. She works for various organizations as a freelance editor, writer and writing facilitator. She is also a film and video curator, especially interested in poetry video.

Charles Rossiter, PhD, CPT is Book Review Editor for the *Journal of Poetry Therapy* and a board member of NAPT. He has received an NEA Fellowship for poetry and hosts the audio website poetrypoetry.com. His recent publications include *Back Beat; Cold Mountain 2000*; and *What Men Talk About*.

Kathleen Adams, LPC, RPT (Foreword/Afterword) is a Registered Poetry/Journal Therapist and the current President of NAPT. She directs the Center for Journal Therapy (www. journaltherapy.com) in Denver, CO and is the author of five books on the power of writing to heal, including the best-selling *Journal to the Self*. She teaches therapeutic writing privately and at universities and hospitals in Colorado.

Thanks to generous donors, copies of *Giving Sorrow Words* have been distributed to New York State victim's assistance counselors and other helping professionals around Manhattan. They are also being used at the Boston Trauma Center with families of victims on flights from Boston on 9/11. In Washington, D.C. they are being used in a variety of counseling contexts. In Tallahassee, Florida, *Giving Sorrow Words* is in use at the Big Bend Hospice and in gri3ef and loss support groups in Colorado Springs, CO; Charleston, SC; Mitchell County, NC; and Glens Falls, NY. In Minneapolis, it is being distributed through the Red Cross to families in their organ and tissue donor program. In Coral Springs, FL, members of the Police and Fire Departments are reading and discussing the book. In Chicago, a theatrical production was based on poems from the book. Copies of the book have been sent to families of the seven astronauts who died aboard the Columbia space shuttle.

Your tax-deductible donation to the NAPT Foundation helps keep this book in print and distributed free of charge to all who need it. Donors of $100 or more receive acknowledgment on this page. Please use the enclosed donation envelope. If the envelope is missing, make your check payable to NAPT Foundation and mail to:

NAPT Foundation
Attn: Giving Sorrow Words
525 SW 5th St., Suite A
Des Moines, IA 50309-4501